## Baseball's Secret and Unwritten Rules

By
Phil Rognier

Illustrator: k.w. kirchner

Copyright ©2005 Phil Rognier

All rights reserved. No part of this publication may be reproduced without the expressed written permission of the publisher, except in the case of brief quotations embodied in critical articles or reviews.

The "rules" have been drawn from the author's contact with baseball the last 50 years, and represent his attempt to share the "wealth".

ISBN: 1-59404-051-6

Printed in Canada

First Printing, January 2005
10 9 8 7 6 5 4 3 2 1

Peanut Butter/Classic Day Publishing
Houseboat #4, 2207 Fairview Ave. E
Seattle, WA 98102
Email: info@classicdaypublishing.com
www.classicdaypublishing.com

Dedicated to REAL baseball people,
those who feel "life is baseball" (and vice versa),
and a wife who endures it!

## ACKNOWLEDGMENTS

To all the people who *love* baseball and have helped maintain its integrity as our national pastime. A special thanks to those who taught me the "rules" of baseball as a coach, mentor, teammate, or fan, and my friends for your support.

To my parents, thank you for encouraging me to play the game and be the BEST I could be. Mom, you "stoked the fire" and understood the passion.

To my wife, Genie, thanks for understanding, supporting, and enduring my love of the game.

To Ivan Moxie, "Catfish the Closer", Uncle Bobbie, Syddd, "Five Fingers" Tony, Jay-son, the Bear, Pooh, 360, Bubba(Yo), "Uncle Max" and all those who *really* love THE GAME.

Special thanks to Elliott Wolf, Kristen Morris, and Peanut Butter Publishing.

P.A.R

# FORWARD
## Ivan Moxie

Everywhere we go and everything we do is governed by laws or rules. It seems to be a compulsive indulgence in our modern society to have a rule for each frame of reference and domain within which we operate. We even have a "rule of thumb" to guide us if we do not have a written, formal, indelible rule or law. It would be great if we only had the Golden Rule to remind us... Then again if everyone followed the Golden Rule we would not need the others... Catch(er)22!

Phil Rognier, a.k.a. Coach Phil, has been in or around baseball for over 50 years...as a player, a parent, coach, manager, teacher, clinician, camp director, and mentor... BUT most importantly as a fan and admirer of our national pastime. His love for the game is unconditional and transcends "normalcy" in that, to him life is baseball. Moreover, he believes that many of "life's little lessons" are learned while playing baseball and the game prepares its young (and old) players for mastering good productive citizenship, parenting, and a successful marriage.

In **THE CODE**, Coach Phil has listed and in some cases illustrated the "secret and unwritten rules" of baseball. These "parameters for proper behavior" have amassed over the past century and a half and although not codified in the official RULES of baseball are considered as important, and to be respected by all participants. **THE CODE** dictates the proper demeanor, attitude, mores, and manners that one should display when involved in the game. In many cases, if one of these unwritten rules is broken there will be a suitable and appropriate punishment bestowed on the miscreant by the opposition as well as fellow players on his team.

**THE CODE** is an amazing "visit" into the inner game of baseball. It will provide average "Joe Fan" insight into the fluency of the game as well as explain many of the homilies, clichés, and other nuances that surround its seemingly complex nature. Other sports are enjoyable but do not have the history, uniqueness nor "secret" rules that govern every action and phase of the game of baseball. Furthermore, football might be as tough as baseball if the ball was thrown at 90 mph to a receiver, basketball if you had only one shot to score, and each could be played with a possible penalty of "chin music", "golden sombrero", and/or "spikes-up" retaliation.

Enjoy this fun look at the secret inner sanctum of baseball and GAGPTH!

~ Ivan Moxie

—— .  . —  —— .  . —— .  —  . . . . !

# "THE CODE"
## *The Real Rules of Baseball*

Life seems to be an environment and state-of-being governed by many rules. The formal rules, or laws, are clearly (in most cases) established and taught to us as we grow up and mature into productive citizens. There are definitive penalties for breaking these laws and can even lead to the loss of life in some cases. We live in a reward-punishment society and it is our choice as to whether we obey the rules or not. One may not claim ignorance of the rules/law because it is our responsibility to know them!!

Besides the formal rules of life, there are the "unwritten rules" of our society. These are not as clear as the formal ones and punishment varies according to the geographic region and the subculture in which one resides. The unwritten rules can be in regard to etiquette, linguistic usage, etc. and be considered simply nuances to the rigid unbreachable mores. They exist everywhere and in some cases and regions are more important that the codified law.

The game of baseball is in many ways a microcosm of "real" life and shares many of its characteristics. Life is not fair and neither is baseball! Many formal rules, enough to fill a rather large tome, have been enacted in order to maintain "fairness" and respect, and as in life, individuals have been appointed in baseball to ensure that the rules are not broken. Also, as in life, there are many **unwritten and secret** rules or what many call the REAL RULES OF BASEBALL, or **"THE CODE"**. Some of these RULES are formal and part of the game but are listed in this book because even though they are written in the rule book, they would be rules nonetheless ....hence, they are unwritten rules that have been "codified" to insure their compliance and guarantee adherence!

Most of **"THE CODE"** was established by real ballplayers throughout the development of the game of baseball in order to keep the game "fair" and "fun". Many reflect concepts neither easily codified nor enforceable; and some are totally based on subjective interpretation. These traditional "rules" have been handed down and established to maintain the integrity of the game and proper decorum among contemporary ball players...to keep the real game intact! In many cases, the unwritten rules change according to the game, where it is played, and/or a situation. As you read and analyze each of the REAL RULES, you will understand the difficulty in enforcing many of these but, on the other hand, if you are a ball player or a true fan you will understand why they are RULES.

In the true baseball culture, "THE CODE" is the rule of law, written or not. These rules are passed down from generation to generation and perpetuated by the denizens of baseball as necessary components to maintain baseball's uniqueness and sense of fairness. A number of the RULES are humorous but arose out of necessity or because someone felt a sense of propriety was needed to guide a particular behavior not listed in the official rule book. By the way, these RULES are neither negotiable nor debatable, and if you feel they are not fair, not equitable ...well, then just like life, baseball is not fair!

"Get a Good Pitch to Hit!"

# THE RULES

Baseball, as life, is NOT fair !

**When in doubt ...
S - L - I - D - E !**

Do not bunt to break up
a no - hitter .
(Ben Davis, hear me ?)

**The only certainty is that the National Anthem is played before the game.**

Do not save a pitcher for tomorrow, it may rain.

When you get a hit, especially a home run, act as if it has happened before.

**A baseball hat does not make a baseball player.**

You **must** make contact on a suicide bunt !

Most one run games are lost, <u>not</u> won.

*Get on base for the next guy.*

# LAW

## The umpire is always right.
(refer to rule : baseball is not fair)

Formula : $U = \dfrac{100\% \, R^2}{1}$

**If you play for one run, that's what you will get.**

There are NO left-handed catchers ... or shortstops ... or second baseman ... or third basemen.

It is as easy to hit a baseball as it is to reduce your nose size.

# Learn to bunt...
# it's as good as a hit !

**ALWAYS hit the cutoff man.**

# YCPBSOYA !!!
### Coach Dennis Denning

**NEVER STEAL WITH A FIVE RUN LEAD AFTER THE SIXTH INNING.**

# LAW

## The odds of striking out are increased by the importance of runners in scoring position.

$$K/\cancel{K} = IROB\,(SP^2)$$

# MOM'S/WOMEN'S RULE

*If a woman has to choose between catching a fly ball AND saving an infant's life,*

*She will choose to save the infant's life without EVEN considering if there are men on base !*

*Dave Barry*

**Baseball acts stand forever, there are NO penalty flags.**

**Good pitching will always stop good hitting and vice versa.**

*Casey Stengel*

**Do not bunt for a base hit when you need a sacrifice bunt.**

# If hit by a pitch NEVER rub the spot ... shake it off !

## A hitter **must** not look back at a catcher's signals while in the batter's box.

## *It 's only a game.*

IT'S "PLAY BALL" **NOT** "WORK BALL"!

A nickname lasts forever.

*Do not play the infield in, early in the game.*

Only use your closer in the late innings with the game on the line.

**Always be 'Heads Up".**

There are NO mulligans or "do - overs" in baseball.

**The fattest guy with the ugliest body will always be the first to take his shirt off.**

Do not go against the percentages.

**The designated hitter must be a POWER hitter.**

Do not use your "stopper" in a tie game; only when you are ahead.

There is <u>NO</u> gambling or steroids in baseball. (*hmmm?*)

The 3 - 0 pitch is <u>not</u> always an automatic strike.

**No Ball   No Game**

Chicks **do** dig the long ball.

Do not hit and run on a 0 - 2 count.

**Do not step on the foul line when going to your defensive position.**

When the catcher drops to block a ball ... take second.

ALWAYS
get the lead runner !

Run EVERYTHING out.

If "dusted" or "brushed back", hit the next pitch through the pitcher's mound.

**Coaches and managers sit in the front of the plane or bus, and players in back.**

not valid in limos.

**It's NOT only a game !**

**Keep your eyes on the ball.**

# Do <u>not</u> bunt
# with a power hitter up.

## The dumbest errors *always* happen in front of a big crowd.

## It ain't over 'til it's over.

*Yogi Berra*

*What happens in the dugout (clubhouse) stays in the dugout (clubhouse).*

**Never swing at a 3-0 pitch (unless the coach green lights you) BUT NEVER EVER if your team has a big lead late in the game.**

*Baseball is 80% mental and 20% mental … yep !*

One great play wipes out 100 bad ones.

**It's not the size of the bat but what you do with it.**

# If you forget to keep your eye on the ball,
# keep your eye on the ball STUPID !

WITH RUNNERS IN SCORING POSITION AND FIRST BASE OPEN, WALK THE 8 BATTER TO PITCH TO THE 9.

**Never look back .**

85% of all
walks (bases on balls) score;
90% of all lead off walks score.

Never discuss a no - hitter
while one is in progress.

Hit 'em where they ain't.

*Wee Willie Keeler*

*Do not "flip" your bat after hitting a home run.*

**If you just signed a contract for more than $15 million you may not say, " it's not about the money".**

*Do not, under any circumstance, fake a tag and make a runner slide.*

**A ball hitting the foul line or foul pole is FAIR.**

The left and right fielders should concede all balls to the centerfielder.

Do not issue an intentional pass (base on balls, walk) if first base is occupied.

Batted balls will ALWAYS find the rookie or the sub.

You must hit a round object (ball) with another round object (bat) SQUARE !

## Always be ready for the curveball.

Shorten up on two strikes as a batter.

**There is NO crying in baseball.**

You can not get picked off home ... or the bench.

Do not let the score influence how you manage.

Rookies "bag the bats"

Never show up an umpire by starting to first base when you have 3 balls and "assume" the pitch was a ball.

**Swing as hard as you can, in case you hit it !**

Never make the first or last out at third base.

If you are not having fun in baseball, you are missing the point.

*Chris Chambliss*

There are NO perfect pitches!

A third strike is <u>not</u> *always* an out.

# LAW

$$FH = EB$$

A "full" head is an empty bat

or (corollary)

$$EH = FB$$

A empty head is a full bat.

**Always have at least one hot dog at the game.**

It takes three
(3, III, tres, trois, tres, 9/3)
outs to end an inning.

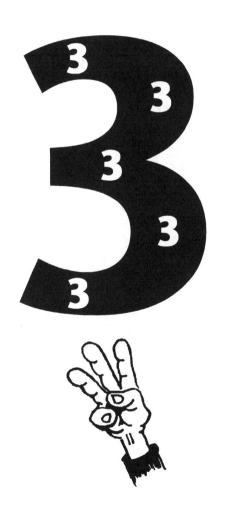

# LAW

$$PTW = N^2TL$$

**Play to win, <u>not</u> to <u>not</u> lose.**

There are over 100 ways to score from third ... get there !

Sometimes a 6" bunt is more powerful than a 400 foot homer.


Left-handed pitchers must wear their hats a "tad" off center.

*Do not question an umpire's heritage, origin of birth, **nor** legitimacy of birth.*

The *longest* balls are hit in batting practice ... or foul.

**Never stand and admire a home run.**

Play like no one is watching.

The **last** hop is always the bad one.

Baseball is unpredictable ... just like life.

Never trust a base runner with a limp.

## You can not hit what you can't see.

ONLY BORING PEOPLE FIND BASEBALL BORING.

Baseball is a game of inches... but you can win with/by feet/feat !

Do not give a team more than three outs in an inning !

NEVER make the first out at home.

# Go down swinging !

*A walk is as good as a hit.*

No team shall "awe" you!

**Hitting is more mental than physical.**

Take a strike when you are behind late in the game.

**It takes NO talent to hustle.**

**Never question an umpire's integrity ... his eyesight ? Yes !**

Even a midget made it to the BIG LEAGUES ... anyone can !

It's a **new** game **everyday.**

Hit the ball where it is pitched!

NEVER charge the mound unless you can back it up.

(Right, Robin Ventura?)

*ALWAYS* wear a cup !!

The Yankees ARE baseball.

**NEVER** throw behind a runner.

*Do not steal when you are two or more runs behind ... or third base with two outs.*

A .120 hitter can beat you as easily as a .350 hitter.

Work is for people who do not play baseball.

ALWAYS swing on a hit-and-run play.

Bunting adds 100 points to your batting average.

**Always take a "good hack".**

# Sometimes 9 <u>innings</u> is a *smidge* too short.

## No "rabbit ears" in baseball.

Never packup the gear/equipment until AFTER the last out and the game is *officially* over.

If you are a pitcher do not, EVER, argue balls and strikes when you are batting.

Play one pitch at a time.

*NEVER squeeze bunt to "mercy rule" an opponent.*

NEVER walk the leadoff hitter or hit him with a pitch ...

There is always a better player aka "The fastest gun theory".

To err is indeed human ... ask any infielder.

## NEVER concede a base to an opponent for ANY reason.

# NO ONE owns the inside 8" of home plate.

# Hitting is as easy as π !

Do not stretch singles into doubles or doubles into triples if you lead by 5 or more runs

A veteran gets away with more than a rookie.

Rhubarb is <u>not</u> always a pie.

**WHEN YOU ARE GREAT, THE PEOPLE WILL TELL YOU.**

# LAW

## Attitude is a MUST to win.

$$A = \frac{GW}{1}$$

You are never
"safe or out by a mile".

If a flyball is hit behind you, tag up and listen to the base coach.

The hands are <u>not</u> always part of the bat.

# Baseball is a pass-fail course... you do or you don't!

# See three balls?
# Hit the middle one!

*Ninety (90) feet between bases is as close to perfection as man has achieved.*

*Red Smith*

If one of your players gets knocked down by a pitch...
**quid pro quo.**
(Hit one of ours, we hit one of yours).
Don Drysdale's corollary: Hit two for every one!

## Baseball is simple but NEVER easy.
*Roger Angell*

## You can't tell the players without a scorecard.

## At Wrigley Field, visitor's home run balls must be thrown back.

When in a "pickle" (rundown) run into the nearest fielder.

Do not sacrifice with your best hitter on deck.

When in doubt choose the GLM (strong little league rule).

**"Chin music" is not always harmonious.**

The game is not over until The LAST out is made.

**Do not bunt on an 0 - 2 count.**

Don't rub it in or run up the score.
(NO R.U.T.S !)

HIT THE BALL, RUN FAST, AND TURN LEFT .....

<u>Never</u> put the tying or go-ahead run on base.

Everyone was a rookie once.

Take the extra base ...
every time!

GAGPTH!

# LAW

$$\frac{3-1+2-1}{1} = HP^2$$

## 2 -1 and 3 -1 counts are BOTH a hitter's pitch !

*Play for the game, not for the fame.*

**Go halfway
on a routine flyball
to the outfield with less than
two outs.**

Never get doubled-up with
nobody out.

## "Freeze" on a line drive.

You do not need luck
IF you are good.

With two outs and a 3-2 count
... as a base runner ...
TAKE OFF !!!

**The harder you work and practice, the "luckier" you get.**

*When runnin' the bases, touch 'em all.*

Each year <u>every</u> player and <u>every</u> team begins at .000.

You ain't NOBODY until you get BOO 'D !

Only a catcher wears his hat backwards.

*When in doubt?*
*Take two and hit to right!*

**Let your bat do the talkin'.**

## CYB not CYA !

**Never let the fear of striking out get in your way.**

*Babe Ruth*

*Do not alibi bad hops, anyone can field good ones.*

**A golden sombrero is <u>not</u> a good thing to wear.**

# NEVER beat yourself !

# You must always get your uniform dirty !

### CATCH THE BALL WITH TWO HANDS !!!

## It is not a simple game.

*With a right hand pitcher on the mound do not walk a right hand batter to pitch to a left hand hitter.*

*Do not show-up the pitcher.*

Under no circumstance should you talk to the opposition ... *hmmm* ?

# Ties do not go to the runner!

Win <u>every</u> inning and you have a "good chance" to win the game.

HARD ball is for HARD guys!

The player making a great defensive play <u>always</u> leads off the next inning when his team is up.

**Anything goes for bench jockeys and their heckling.**

Slide HARD !!

Unwritten rules are just as *inportant* as written rules ... and there are **more** of them.

_____ (Your secret or unwritten rule. See last page to include in "The Code Deux")

## ENJOY THE GAME .....
## ALWAYS !

# KNOW THE RULES

*written or unwritten !!*

## ... and in th' bottom of the ninth, with two outs, the bases loaded, and with a full count ...

(TO BE CONTINUED)

# THE FIRSTSWING FOUNDATION

Phil Rognier is the Executive Director of the FirstSwing Foundation, a Washington state nonprofit corporation. FirstSwing's mission is to teach young ballplayers "life's little lessons" within a baseball/softball environment, and to view the game(s) as a *process* NOT an end in itself. One of the Foundation's most important priorities is to provide physically and financially-challenged youngsters an opportunity to enjoy a baseball experience which will empower them to be successful in their future endeavors. Our FirstSwing camps and clinics (www.firstswingcamps.com) and corporation are dedicated to that mission.

Thank you for your support and commitment to our cause.

Donations may be sent to: FIRSTSWING
P.O. Box 497
Medina, WA 98039

If you know and wish to share your own unwritten rule please send it to FirstSwing and we will include it in our next CODE.
firstswing36@hotmail.com

## EXTRA INNINGS TO FOLLOW

Look for "the Code Deux" !!!
more secret rules
and

## "Life's Little Lessons" by Phil Rognier

A compendium of articles, statements, and insights by "various and sundry" individuals as to what THEY learned about life from the game of baseball. Includes everyone from the President, to ex-ball players, to housewives, to business people, to parents...It is more than just a game!